P9-DBS-468

ROY HALLADAY

BY ALEX MONNIG

Printed in the United States of America,
North Mankato, Minnesota
092011
012012

♻ THIS BOOK CONTAINS AT LEAST 10% RECYCLED MATERIALS.

Editor: Chrös McDougall
Copy Editor: Anna Comstock
Series Design: Craig Hinton
Cover and Interior Production: Kazuko Collins

Photo Credits: Matt Slocum/AP Images, cover, 1, 29; Rob Carr/AP Images, 4; Eric Gay/AP
Images, 7; Frank Gunn/AP Images, 8; Matt Rourke/AP Images, 11; Scott Halleran/Allsport/
Getty Images, 12; Peter Muhly/AFP/Getty Images, 14; Ed Zurga/AP Images, 17; Paul
Sancya/AP Images, 18; Matthew Stockman/Getty Images, 21; Steve Nesius/AP Images,
23; Nathan Denette/The Canadian Press/AP Images, 24; Mel Evans/AP Images, 27

Library of Congress Cataloging-in-Publication Data

Monnig, Alex.
  Roy Halladay : superstar pitcher / by Alex Monnig.
     p. cm. — (Playmakers)
  Includes bibliographical references and index.
  ISBN 978-1-61783-291-8
  1. Halladay, Roy, 1977—Juvenile literature. 2. Baseball players—United
States—Biography—Juvenile literature. 3. Pitchers (Baseball—United States—
Biography—Juvenile literature. I. Title.
  GV865.H233M67 2012
  796.357092—dc23
  [B]
                                    2011038899

TABLE OF CONTENTS

Roy Halladay

DAZZLING DEBUT

Roy Halladay had long been a top pitcher in Major League Baseball (MLB). But he was hardly the most well known. In 12 seasons with the Toronto Blue Jays, he never pitched in the playoffs. That changed in 2010. The Philadelphia Phillies traded for Roy that year. They were the defending World Series champions.

Roy starred on the bigger stage. He threw a perfect game during the regular season. It was only

Roy Halladay hugs catcher Carlos Ruiz after throwing a no-hitter in his first career playoff game in 2010.

the 20th perfect game in the history of MLB. Roy also got a chance to pitch in the playoffs. He made history there too.

The Phillies played the Cincinnati Reds in the first round of the playoffs. Roy was on the mound for Game 1. After eight innings, only one Reds player had gotten on base. Roy had walked him in the fifth inning.

Roy then got all three Reds batters out in order in the bottom of the ninth inning. That completed the no-hitter. MLB had been around for more than 100 years. Yet that was only the second time a pitcher threw a no-hitter in the postseason.

Those who knew Roy when he was young were not surprised to see his success. Roy was born on May 14, 1977, in Denver, Colorado. And he was passionate about baseball from an early age.

Roy's father encouraged him. The family moved to a new home when Roy was young. His father built a batting cage in the basement. It included a pitching mound. That was where Roy learned to pitch. Roy quickly fell in love with baseball. He practiced whenever he could. And when he was not practicing, Roy read about baseball.

Roy signs autographs for fans during spring training in 2011. He became more recognizable on the winning Phillies.

One of his favorite books was Nolan Ryan's handbook. Ryan was a Hall of Fame pitcher known for throwing the ball very hard. Roy wanted to be just like Ryan someday.

Roy grew into a baseball star at Arvada West High School. He made the All-State team three years in a row. And he was named the state's Most Valuable Player twice. By his high school graduation, MLB teams had taken notice.

Roy Halladay

CHAPTER 2

MINOR DEVELOPMENTS

Roy Halladay graduated from high school in 1995. The 1995 MLB Draft was that summer. The Toronto Blue Jays selected Halladay 17th. Very few professional baseball players start their careers in the majors. And Halladay was no different. He began his pro career in the rookie league.

Halladay pitched only 50 1/3 innings that season. But he showed signs of a bright future. His earned-run

Halladay had to work his way up through the minor leagues before he could pitch for the Toronto Blue Jays.

average (ERA) was 3.40. That meant he gave up only 3.4 runs per nine innings. Halladay also struck out 48 batters that season.

Halladay continued to get better. So the Blue Jays quickly moved him through the minors. He reached Class AAA in 1997. That is the division just under the major leagues.

Halladay began the 1998 season in Class AAA. He was not striking out batters like he had in 1995. But the Blue Jays were still impressed with his pitching. So they called him up to the major leagues.

Halladay pitched his first major league game on September 20, 1998. He was just 21 years old. That made him the third youngest pitcher to ever start a game for the Blue Jays. He pitched against the Tampa Bay Devil Rays. It was an average start. Halladay threw for five innings. He gave up eight hits and allowed three runs.

Halladay was working out at a gym in Colorado one day in 1997. A young woman named Brandy came over to talk to him. She had been friends with Halladay's older sister. He called Brandy later that night, and they started dating. She later became his wife.

Former Phillies pitcher Jim Bunning, *left*, greets the Halladays: Roy, his wife Brandy, and their sons Braden and Ryan.

It was his second start that really got people excited. Halladay came just one out away from throwing a no-hitter against the Detroit Tigers. He gave up his first hit with two outs in the ninth inning. Many great pitchers never throw a no-hitter in their careers. Halladay had almost done it in his second start. The Blue Jays' rookie appeared to be on a path to stardom. But there would be some bumps in the road before he got there.

Roy Halladay

CHAPTER 3

ROY'S ROUGH RUN

Roy Halladay pitched in two major league games in 1998. But he had shown lots of promise. So the Blue Jays started him in the majors in 1999. And he stayed there all season.

It was a learning experience for the pitcher. The Blue Jays finished third in the American League (AL) East Division. Halladay pitched in 36 games. Half of those were as a starting pitcher while the other half were as a relief pitcher.

Halladay throws a pitch during spring training in 1998. He made his major league debut that year.

Blue Jays pitching coach Mel Queen watches Roger Clemens practice. Queen helped Halladay regain his form in 2001.

Halladay had an 8–7 record that season. People were more impressed with his 3.92 ERA and 82 strikeouts. Those were solid numbers for a first-year player. But the news was not all good. Halladay also walked 79 batters. It is not a good sign when pitchers walk nearly as many hitters as they strike out.

Walking so many batters also hurt him in 2000. Halladay got rocked. He had a 10.64 ERA in 67.2 innings. He walked 42 hitters and only struck out 44. At the time, it was the worst ERA of any pitcher to ever throw at least 60 innings in one season. Toronto had no choice but to send Halladay back down to the minors. But he continued to struggle in Class AAA. Halladay had a 5.50 ERA in 73.2 innings.

Halladay had the look of a future star in 1998. But he looked like he might be a bust by 2001. At one point that season, the Blue Jays sent him back to Class A. That is three levels beneath the majors.

It was a difficult time for Halladay. He was upset and embarrassed. Pitching had always come so easily for him. He began to have doubts about whether he would ever make it back to MLB. And he was just 24 years old. At one point, he even asked his wife if they had enough money for him to instead go to college.

Halladay decided to keep a journal when he was struggling with his pitching. He kept track of all the workouts and drills he did. The journal helped him return to form. Halladay continued writing in a journal even after he became one of baseball's top pitchers.

But Halladay stuck with baseball. He soon began working with pitching coach Mel Queen. Queen wanted Halladay to go back to basics. That meant not even pitching in games. And at first, Queen did not even let Halladay throw an actual ball. The two just focused on Halladay's throwing motion and grip.

The results were incredible. Halladay's fastball showed more movement. That made it much harder to hit. Halladay also learned to throw over the plate more often. That helped him cut down on his walks.

Soon the Blue Jays brought him up to Class AA. He pitched 34 innings and had a 2.12 ERA there. More importantly, he struck out 29 batters and only walked six. The Blue Jays then moved him up to Class AAA. He continued to pitch well there. Halladay pitched 14 innings. He struck out 13 hitters while walking none.

"I think it says a lot about his mental toughness. What Roy did says a lot, to take not one step backward but multiple steps backward. A lot of kids would have folded their tents." —Former Phillies scout Mike Arbuckle on Halladay's fall and rise through the minors

Halladay throws a pitch during a 2002 game. He struggled in 2001 and had to go back to the minors.

The Blue Jays took notice. They called Halladay back to the major leagues. And he continued to roll there. Halladay ended the season with 105.1 innings in the majors. He had 96 strikeouts and only 25 walks in that time. And his ERA was only 3.16. The old Halladay was back and better than ever. And he would never again have to go back to the minor leagues.

Roy Halladay

CHAPTER 4

DOC'S DOMINANCE

Roy Halladay had his confidence back. In 2002, he had his first full year as a starting pitcher in MLB. And it was a great one. He was just 25 years old. But he led the league in innings pitched with 239.1. He finished with a 19–7 record. And he was selected for his first All-Star Game.

Tom Cheek was the Blue Jays' radio announcer for many years. He began referring to the team's new ace pitcher as "Doc" Halladay in 2002. The name was

Halladay throws a pitch to a Detroit Tigers hitter during a 2002 game.

Halladay considered quitting baseball in 2001. His wife Brandy bought some books to help him during the hard times. One of those books was *The Mental ABC's of Pitching* by H. A. Dorfman. Halladay liked the book so much that he met with Dorfman in 2002. The book helped rebuild Halladay's confidence.

a tribute to Doc Holliday. He was a famous cowboy who was known for his skills shooting guns.

Halladay went 22–7 in 2003. That was the best record in MLB. Halladay did more than win, though. He had a 3.25 ERA, 204 strikeouts, and just 32 walks. Halladay also had nine complete games that year. That tied him for the MLB lead.

Still, the Blue Jays continued to be just an average team. They had a winning record in 2003. But they were still not close to making the playoffs. Halladay's pitching did not go unnoticed, though. He again made the AL All-Star team that year. But the bigger honor came after the season. Halladay won his first Cy Young Award. That award is given every year to the top pitcher in each league.

Over the years, Halladay had become known for his intense workouts. He continued those habits after winning

Halladay, *with beard*, stands with teammates for the national anthem at the 2003 All-Star Game.

the Cy Young Award. He wanted to get even better. But he might have pushed himself too hard in 2004.

Halladay's shoulder began to hurt that season. It was so bad at times that he could not even pitch. The Blue Jays had to place Halladay on the disabled list twice that season. It was a frustrating season for Halladay. He only pitched in 21 games. The year before he had pitched in 36.

There was even more disappointment for Halladay and the Blue Jays in 2005. Halladay started the season great. After 19 starts, he had a 12–4 record with a 2.41 ERA. He was even selected as a starting pitcher at the All-Star Game. But Halladay never got that chance. He was pitching two days before the All-Star Game when a line drive hit his leg and broke it. Halladay missed the rest of the season. Meanwhile, the Blue Jays finished with another losing record.

Halladay worked hard to get healthy. He also used some of his free time to focus on other things. Halladay and his wife Brandy started a charity program that year called Doc's Box. They bought a private suite in Toronto's home stadium. The Halladays invited sick children and members of local youth groups to come to games for free. The kids even got to visit the field during batting practice. Halladay later moved the program to Philadelphia when he joined the Phillies.

Texas Rangers outfielder Kevin Mench hit the line drive that broke Halladay's leg in 2005. Halladay fell to the ground in pain. But he still picked up the ball and threw out Mench at first.

Blue Jays catcher Bengie Molina, *left*, congratulates Halladay after Halladay pitched a complete game in 2006.

The Blue Jays were happy with Halladay's performance over the years. They felt he would be a key to them finally making the playoffs. So they signed him to a three-year contract extension before the 2006 season. Halladay continued to pitch well for the Blue Jays. But starting pitchers only play in approximately one of every five games. He would need some help if the Blue Jays were to return to the playoffs.

Roy Halladay

CHAPTER 5

POSTSEASON PUSH

Roy Halladay was finally injury free in 2006. And he went right back to All-Star form. He went 16–5 in 32 starts. Halladay also had a 3.19 ERA with 132 strikeouts and only 34 walks. That was enough to place him third in Cy Young Award voting. But it was not enough to help his team make the playoffs. Toronto finished second in its division.

The next three years would be more of the same. Halladay kept pitching well. He never had

Halladay pitches to the Los Angeles Angels of Anaheim during a 2009 game. It was his last season in Toronto.

less than 16 wins from 2007 to 2009. He also led the league in complete games during each of those years. And Halladay was selected as an All-Star in 2008 and 2009. But Toronto still failed to make the playoffs year after year. The Blue Jays' last playoff appearance had been in 1993, when they won the World Series.

Halladay badly wanted to win a World Series one day too. There was little question that he was one of baseball's top pitchers. But the Blue Jays realized they were not close to a World Series title. So they decided to trade Halladay. He could go to a team that had a better chance of winning a World Series. In return, the Blue Jays could get many cheap, young players.

Toronto sent Halladay to the Philadelphia Phillies before the 2010 season. The pitcher quickly adapted to the National League (NL). And the Phillies even selected him to be their

Halladay was happy to be traded to a contending team in 2010. But he was also sad to leave Toronto. Halladay bought a full-page advertisement in a Toronto newspaper. It thanked the Blue Jays and their fans for their support during his 15 years in Toronto.

After 13 seasons in the majors, Halladay threw a no-hitter in his first career postseason start in 2010.

Opening Day starter that season. He pitched seven innings on Opening Day, striking out nine batters and allowing just one run. It was the first of many wins for Halladay that year.

He won an NL-high 21 games that season. He also led the league in complete games, shutouts, and innings pitched. Halladay was again selected for the All-Star Game. And he won his second Cy Young Award.

Halladay had started 320 games without pitching in the playoffs. But he finally got that opportunity in 2010. The Phillies were the defending NL champions. And their chances of a return to the World Series looked good after Halladay's no-hitter victory in the opening game of the playoffs.

The Phillies swept the Cincinnati Reds in the first round. But they met their match in the NL Championship Series. Halladay pitched well in his two games. But the San Francisco Giants beat the Phillies four games to two. And the Phillies' season was over.

Phillies fans had reason to be excited going into 2011. Halladay had won the NL Cy Young Award in 2010. The team also had other talented pitchers such as Cole Hamels and Roy Oswalt. Then the Phillies added another star pitcher named Cliff Lee. He had won the 2008 AL Cy Young Award. Fans wondered if anybody could stop the Phillies in 2011.

Halladay was still the ace of Philadelphia's staff. He won 19 games that season. His ERA was just 2.35. Many believed he was again the best pitcher in the NL. The Phillies lived up to the hype too. Their 102 wins were the most of any MLB team.

Halladay gave up one run in eight innings during Game 5 of the 2011 NL Division Series, but the Phillies lost 1–0.

Halladay said he was confident the Phillies could beat any team in the postseason. But it was not to be. Halladay opened the playoffs with a win over the St. Louis Cardinals. He only allowed one run in Game 5. But the Phillies lost the game and the series. It was a disappointing end to an exciting season. Still, after waiting 13 years to get to the postseason, Halladay had shown he still belonged with the best of the best.

FUN FACTS AND QUOTES

- The Phillies had a chance to select Roy Halladay with the 14th selection in the 1995 MLB Draft. But they instead chose outfielder Reggie Taylor. He played briefly for the Phillies in the early 2000s, but he didn't experience Halladay's success. The Phillies finally got their man 15 years later when they traded for Halladay.

- Even though he is very serious about his dedication to pitching, Halladay has always been a bit of a jokester. He did standup comedy in his elementary school talent show. And he scared his coach by wearing a fake cast before the high school state baseball tournament.

- Halladay and his wife Brandy have two sons named Braden and Ryan.

- *Nolan Ryan's Pitcher's Bible* helped Halladay become a star pitcher growing up. Ryan became one of Halladay's heroes. He even named one of his sons, Ryan, after the famous pitcher.

- Halladay was also a talented basketball player in high school. He was voted second team All-State as a center. He was even offered a partial scholarship to play basketball in college.

WEB LINKS

To learn more about Roy Halladay, visit ABDO Publishing Company online at **www.abdopublishing.com**. Web sites about Halladay are featured on our Book Links page. These links are routinely monitored and updated to provide the most current information available.

GLOSSARY

ace

The best starting pitcher on a team's pitching staff.

disabled list

A list of players who are injured and unable to play in games.

draft

When MLB teams select players in high school and college to come play on their team.

line drive

A ball that is hit hard and flat in the air.

minor leagues

The lower divisions that developing baseball players compete in before they are ready to play in the major leagues.

no-hitter

A game in which a pitcher does not allow the other team to get a hit.

perfect game

A game in which the opposing team does not get any runners on base.

playoffs

A tournament at the end of the year that decides who will win the championship.

relief pitcher

A substitute who is brought in to take over pitching duties from the starting pitcher.

rookie

A first-year player in MLB.

shutouts

Games in which a pitcher holds the opposing team scoreless.

starting pitcher

The pitcher who is chosen to start a baseball game for his team.

suite

A private room at a ballpark in which a group of fans can watch a game.

INDEX

FURTHER RESOURCES

Gerstner, Joanne. *Toronto Blue Jays*. Edina, MN: ABDO Publishing Co., 2011.

Jackson, Dave. *Philadelphia Phillies*. Edina, MN: ABDO Publishing Co., 2011.

Kurtz, Paul. *162–0: A Phillies Perfect Season*. Chicago, IL: Triumph Books, 2011.